ANA, NAB A B

A SIL, SIDES REVERSED, IS LISA.

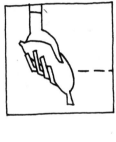

M000002268

ANA, NAB A BANANA

A BOOK OF PALINDROMES

BY
CRAIG HANSEN

A PLUME BOOK

For
Mom and Dad, my two favorite palindromes,
Jenny,
and Dorfdarb the Invincible

PLUME • Published by the Penguin Group • Penguin Books USA Inc., 375 Hudson Street, New York, New York 10014, U.S.A. • Penguin Books Ltd, 27 Wrights Lane, London W8 5TZ, England • Penguin Books Australia Ltd, Ringwood, Victoria, Australia • Penguin Books Canada Ltd, 10 Alcorn Avenue, Toronto, Ontario, Canada M4V 3B2 • Penguin Books (N.Z.) Ltd, 182-190 Wairau Road, Auckland 10, New Zealand • Penguin Books Ltd, Registered Offices: Harmondsworth, Middlesex, England • First published by Plume, an imprint of Dutton Signet, a division of Penguin Books USA Inc. • First Printing, June, 1995

10 9 8 7 6 5 4 3 2 1

Copyright © Craig Hansen, 1995 • All rights reserved • ℗ REGISTERED TRADEMARK — MARCA REGISTRADA • Printed in the United States of America • Without limiting the rights under copyright reserved above, no part of this publication may be reproduced, stored in or introduced into a retrieval system, or transmitted, in any form, or by any means (electronic, mechanical, photocopying, recording, or otherwise), without the prior written permission of both the copyright owner and the above publisher of this book. • BOOKS ARE AVAILABLE AT QUANTITY DISCOUNTS WHEN USED TO PROMOTE PRODUCTS OR SERVICES. FOR INFORMATION PLEASE WRITE TO PREMIUM MARKETING DIVISION, PENGUIN BOOKS USA INC., 375 HUDSON STREET, NEW YORK, NY 10014.

INTRODUCTION

The first palindrome I ever composed — I think I was twelve years old at the time — was Tons o' snot. Be glad I wasn't inspired to illustrate that one. It was only a few years before that juvenile attempt that I first learned what a palindrome was.

In fourth grade, at the Fig Garden Elementary School library I checked out a book called *Perplexing Puzzles and Tantalizing Teasers*. Among the mazes and riddles and tricks with dollar bills were two pages of palindromes: words, phrases, and sentences which read the same backward as forward. I remember lying on my stomach, on the black and white shag carpet of our living room floor, propped up on my elbows, and staring in wonder at the palindrome:

A man, a plan, a canal — Panama!

I was confounded. I gaped. I said, in a fourth-grade voice full of awe, "No way!" The sentence before me defied comprehension, like a magic trick, a high-wire act: it was impossible, but there it was.

"How does a person write a sentence like that? Where do you start?" My brain knotted.

Twenty years passed, and in that time, through many failed and confused attempts, I finally acquired the notable and useless ability to write palindromes.

Occasionally, people ask me how I do it. The short, Zen-like answer is: Begin in the center and grow outward. The long answer is: Mess around on Dad's expensive reel-to-reel tape recorder and listen to yourself talking backward, play Hangman and Hinky-Pinky and the Car Trip Alphabet game, laugh at your family's puns — most of which are funny, study your book of M. C. Escher drawings and listen to Spike Jones records at the same time, learn magic tricks, make Moebius strips, build card houses, invent new words with Scrabble letters, and, particularly, have an older brother who composes dozens of twisted little palindromes to inspire you through jealousy.

That's what worked for me. If you decide to try your hand at palindroming, you'll find your own strange reservoir of inspiration. And keep in mind that all possible palindromes already exist out there, somewhere, by implication, and that writing them is less an act of invention than it is of discovery.

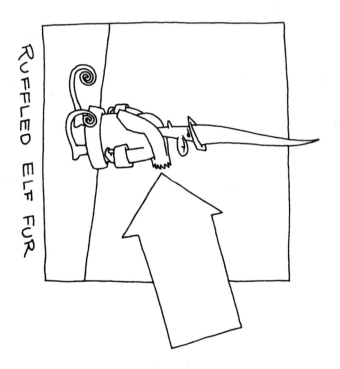

RUFFLED ELF FUR

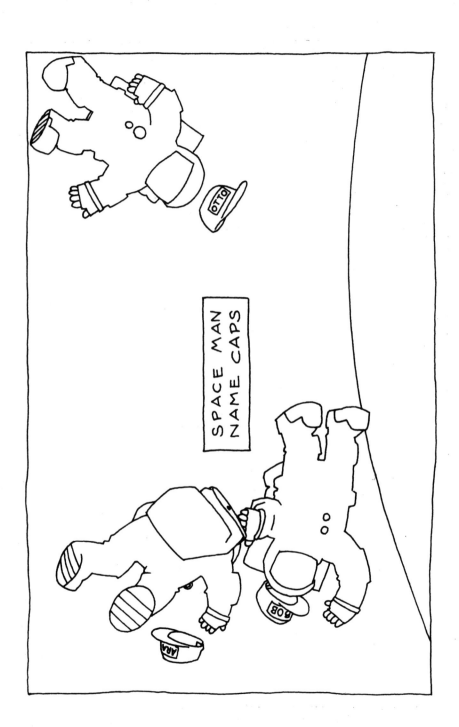

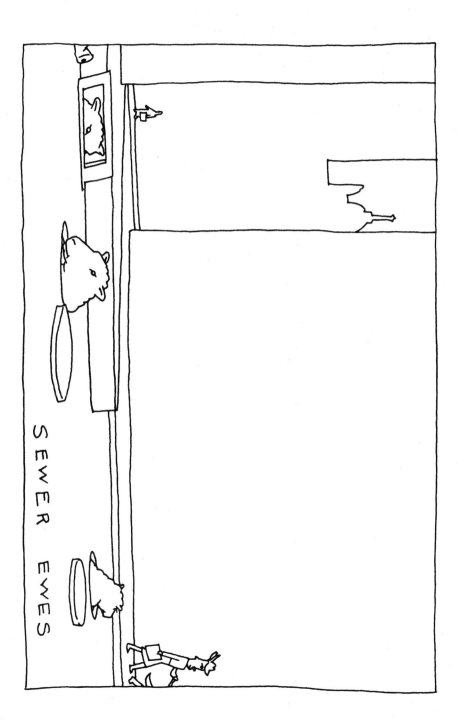

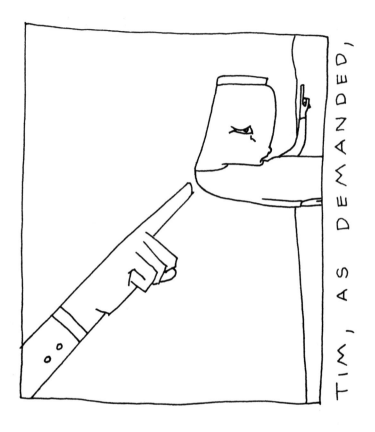

TIM, AS DEMANDED,

NAMED SAM "IT".

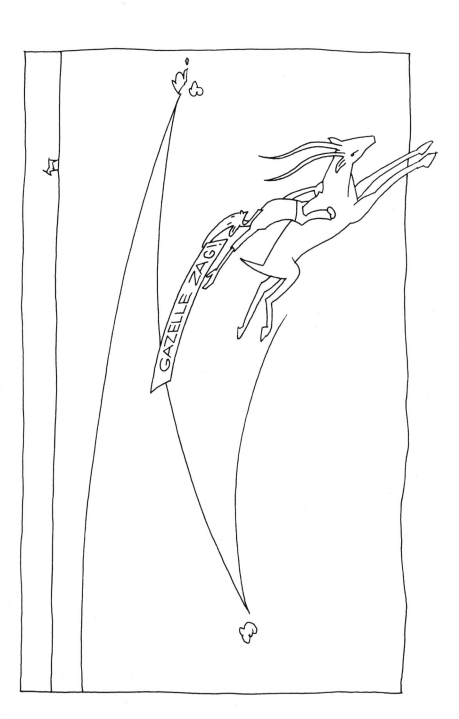

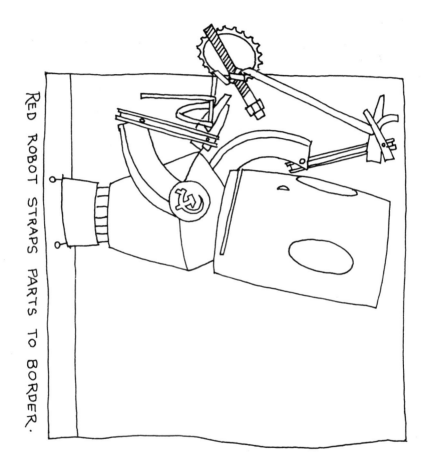

RED ROBOT STRAPS PARTS TO BORDER.

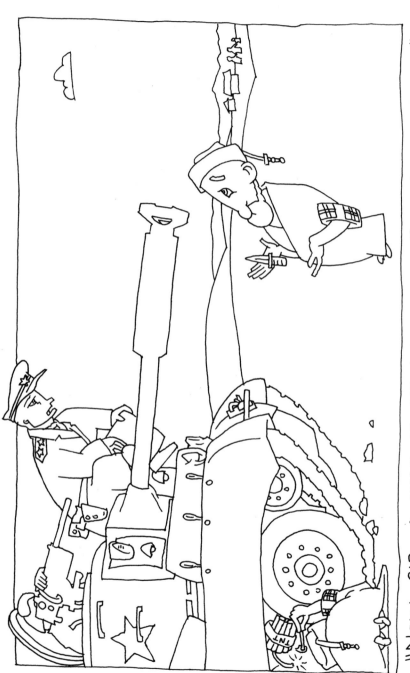

"Now sir, a war is never even. Sir, a war is won."

"DALE — IT'S A PASTIE, LAD."

"TAPE LIVER TO HIS EYES!!!
TAPE PAT'S EYES!! I, HOT, REVILE PAT!"

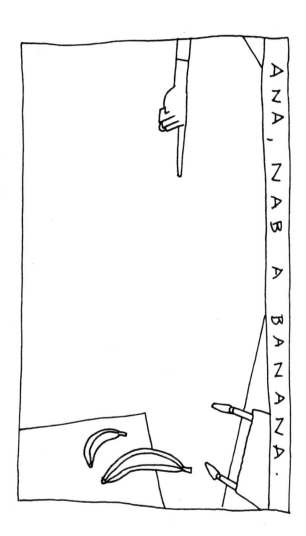

ANA, NABA BANANA.

SNACK CANS!

LEG GEL!

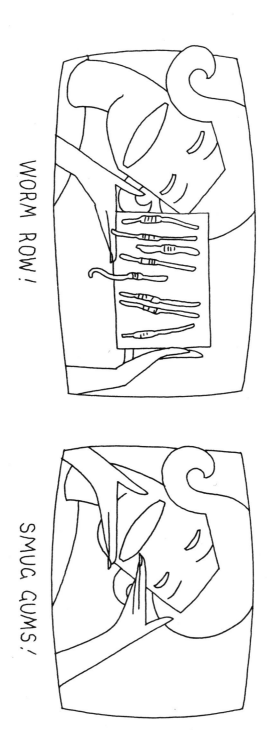

"MA IS ACIDIC, AS I AM."

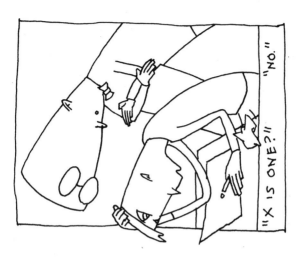

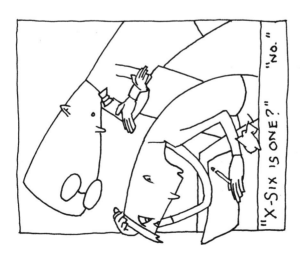

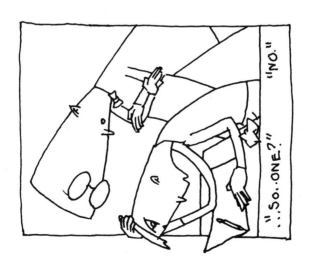

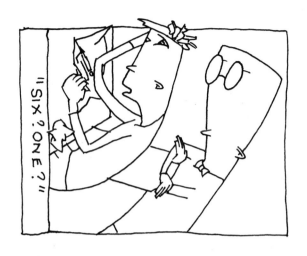

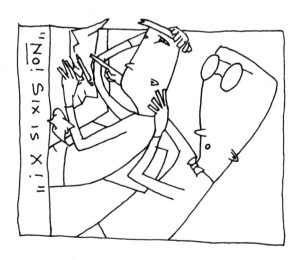

DIARY RAID

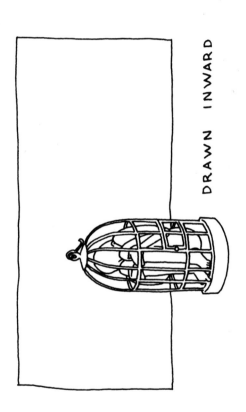

DRAWN INWARD

DEVIL, ON A CLOVEN OLD LONE VOLCANO, LIVED.

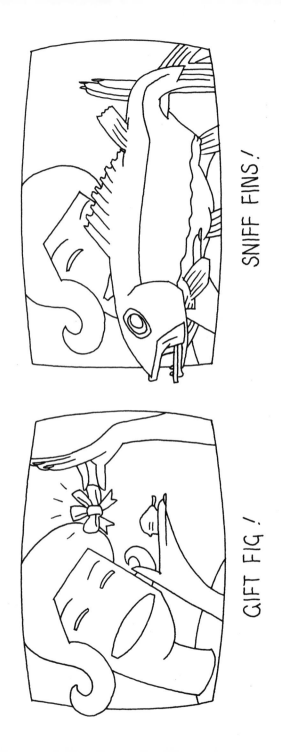

SNIFF FINS!

GIFT FIG!

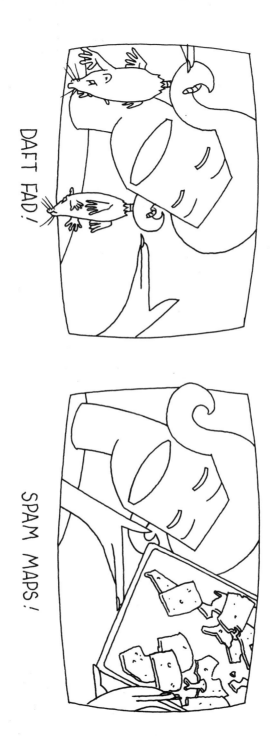

SoRE, HoT LoVERS; REVOLT!

...oH EROS....

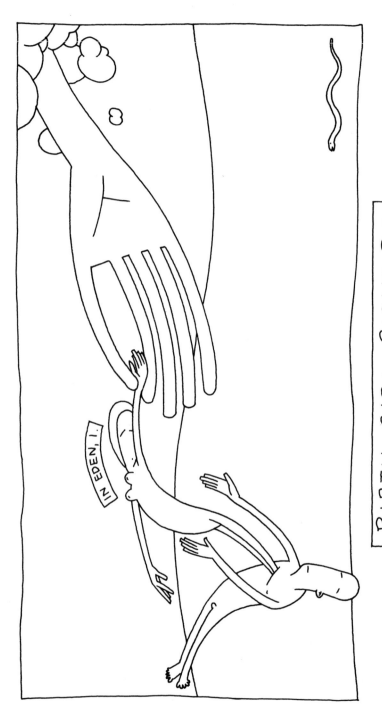

IN EDEN, I.

BIRTH GIRL RIGHT RIB

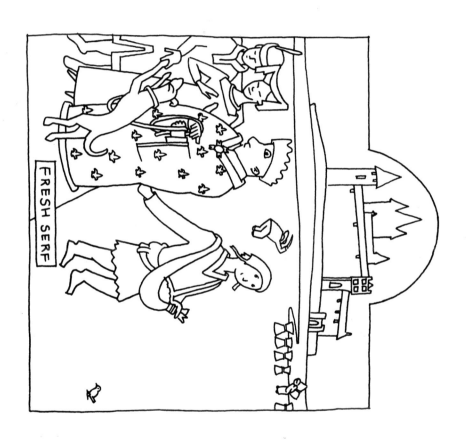

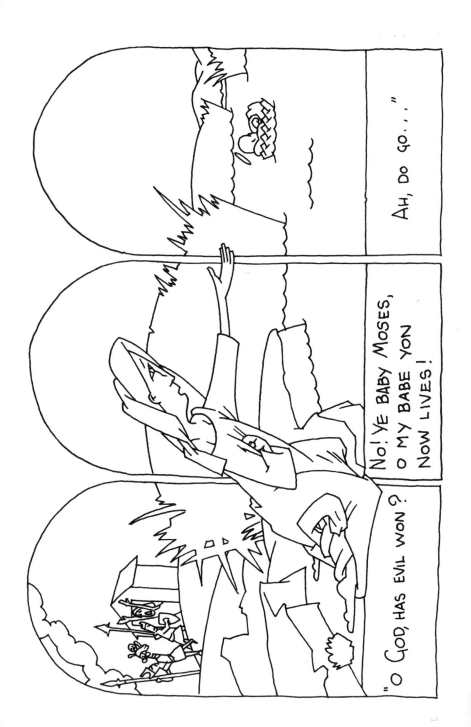

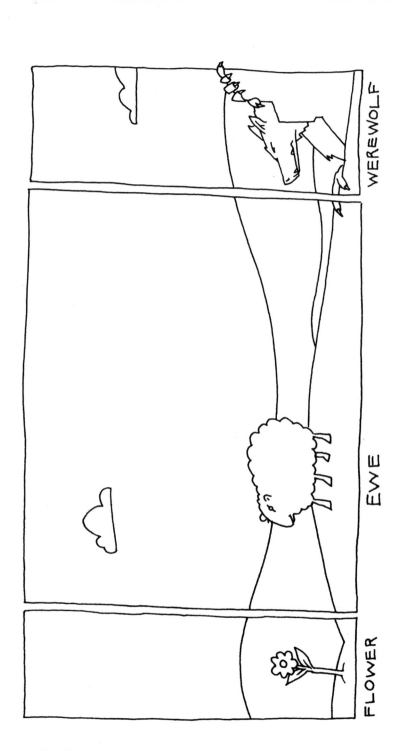

FLOWER

EWE

WEREWOLF

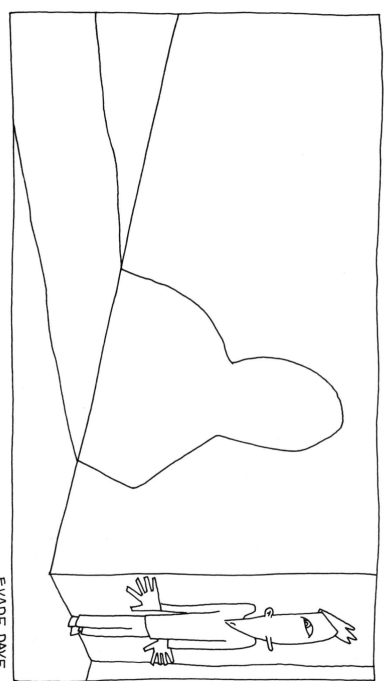

EVADE DAVE.

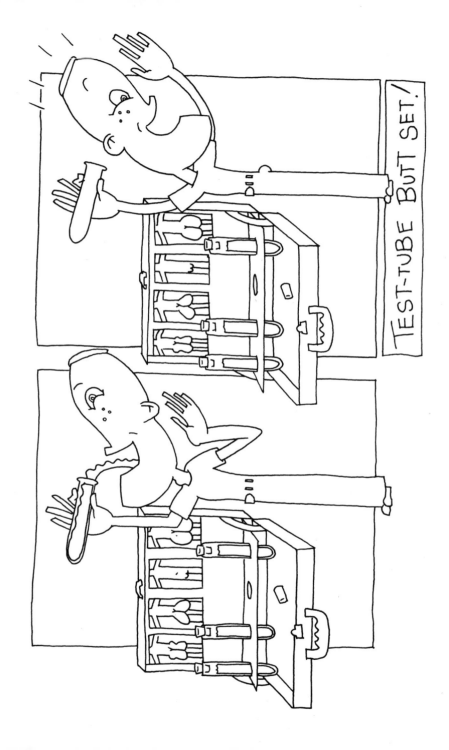

TEST-TUBE BUTT SET!

TACO CAT!

SLEEK EELS!

TINY NIT!

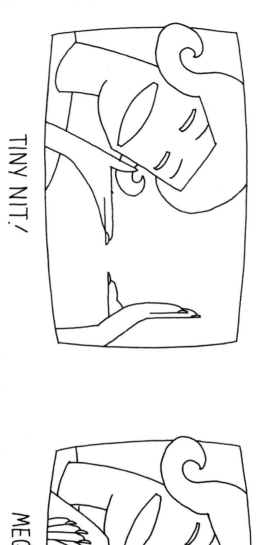

MEGA GEM!

MADAM EVA'S STEPS RETRACED!
AL "BLADE" CARTER'S PETS SAVE MADAM

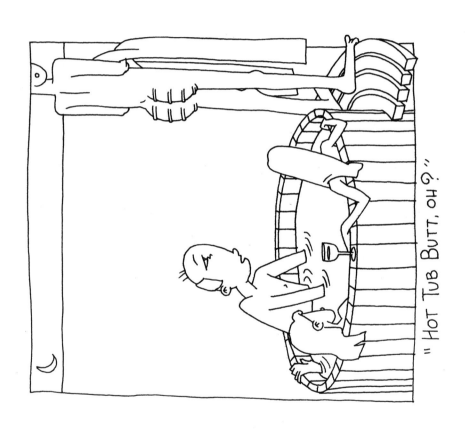

" Hot Tub Butt, oh ? "

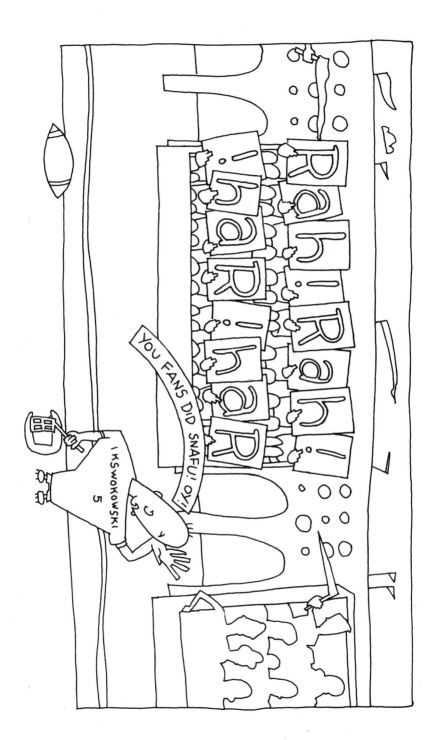

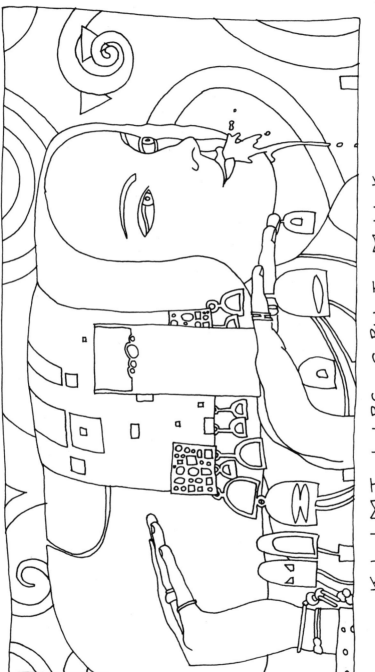

KLIMT LIPS SPILT MILK.

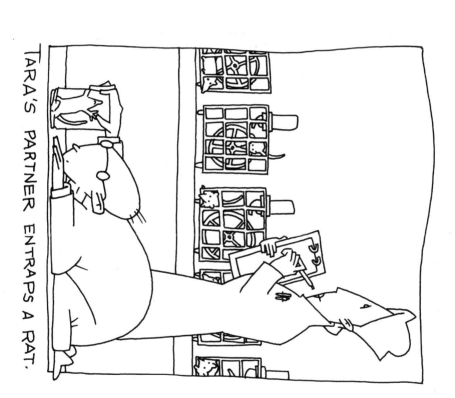

TARA'S PARTNER ENTRAPS A RAT.

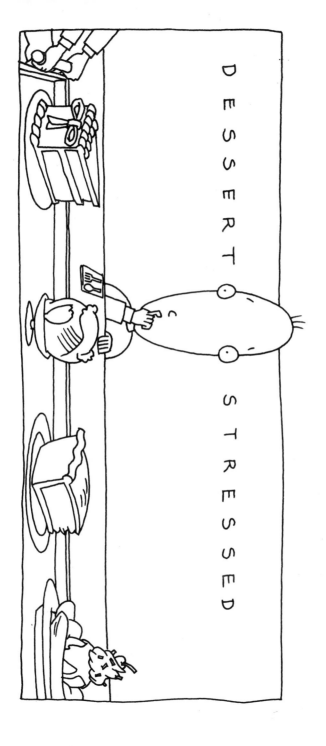

DESSERT

STRESSED

PAGE GAP

"RAM AT NINETY APIECE? I PAY TEN IN TAMAR!"

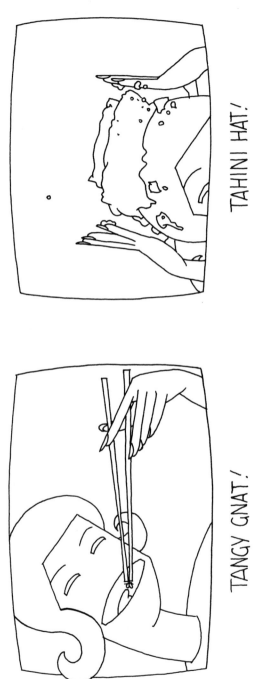

TANGY GNAT!

TAHINI HAT!

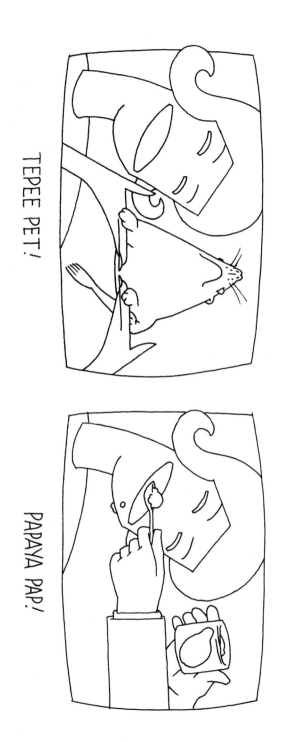

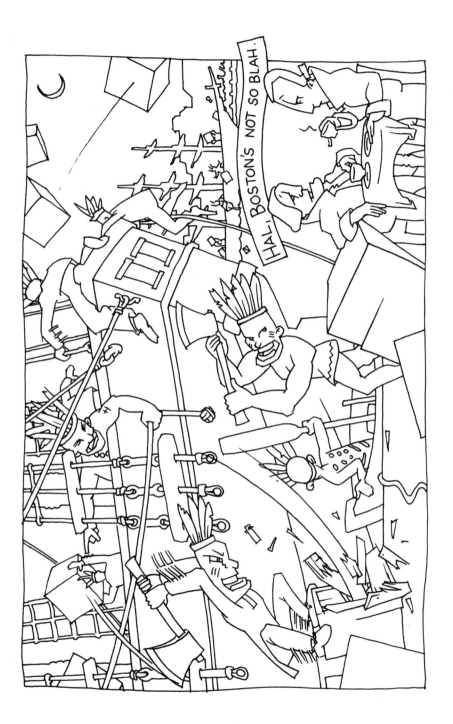

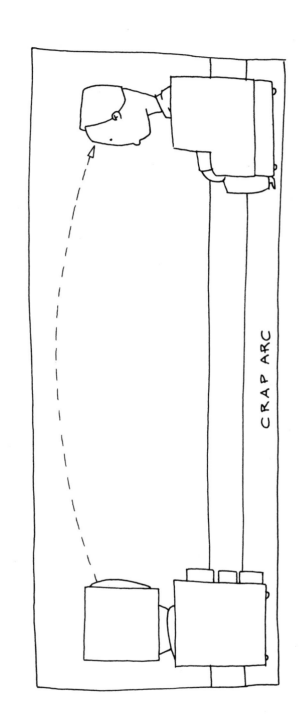

CRAP ARC

To sleep, O ogre! Vile mongrel! Dip ass, sap! Idler! Gnome! Liver goop! Eel! Sot!

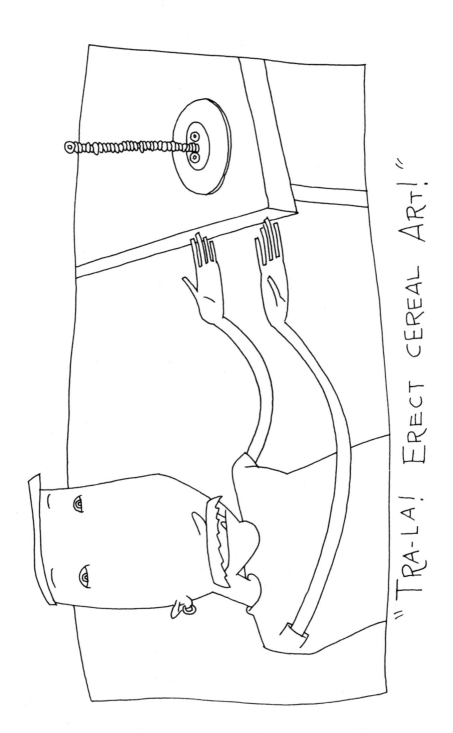

"TRA-LA! ERECT CEREAL ART!"

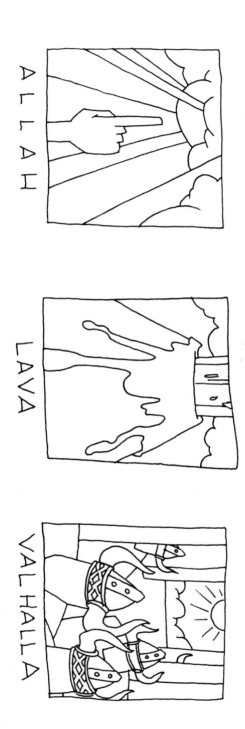

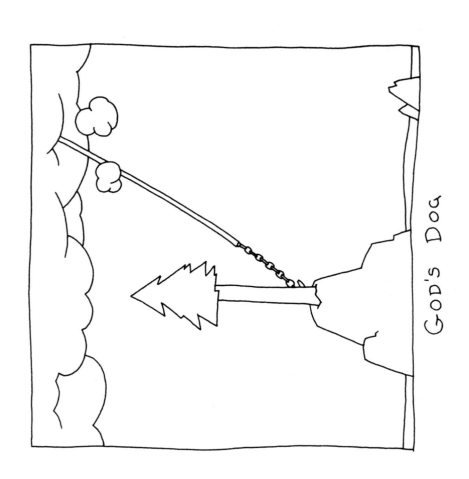

GOD'S DOG

NAT'S DEN NABBED A DEB, BANNED STAN.

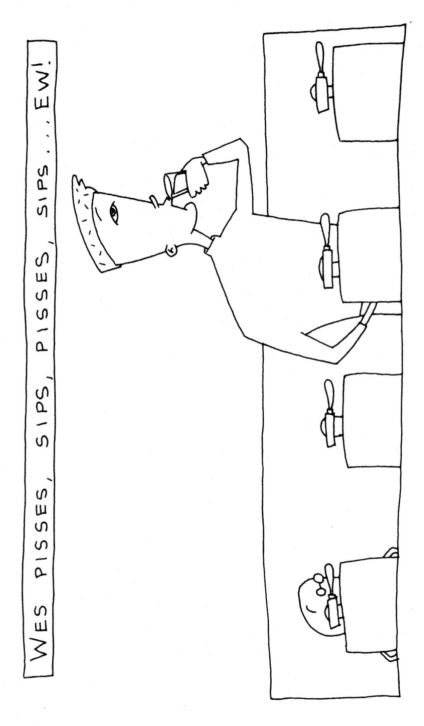

WES PISSES, SIPS, PISSES, SIPS...EW!

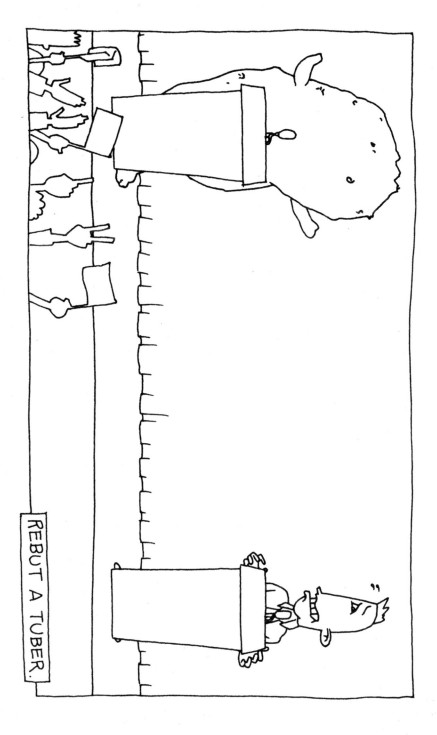

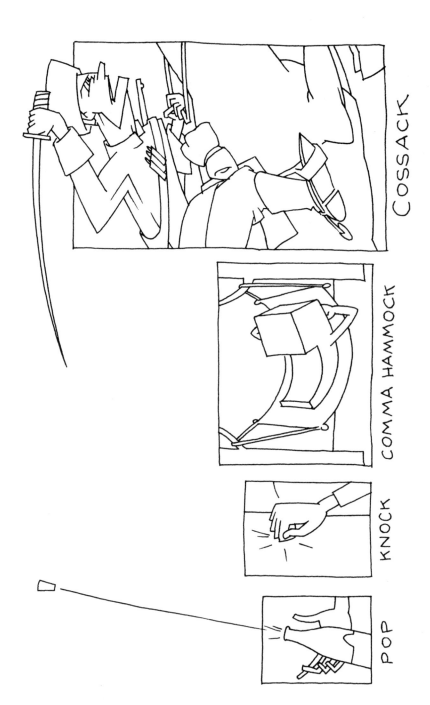

COSSACK

COMMA HAMMOCK

KNOCK

POP

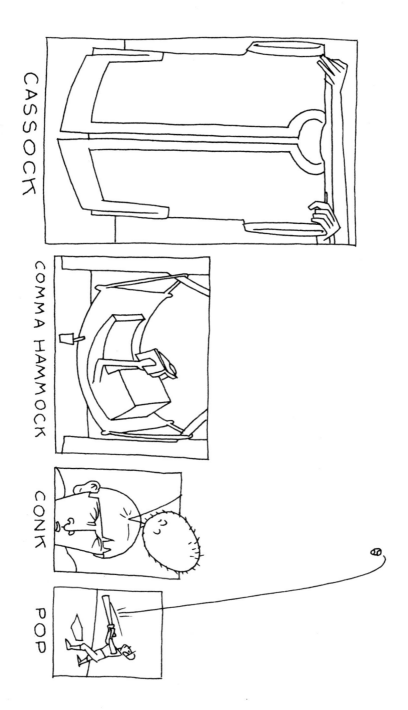

RESALE LASER!

LEVON'S NOVEL!

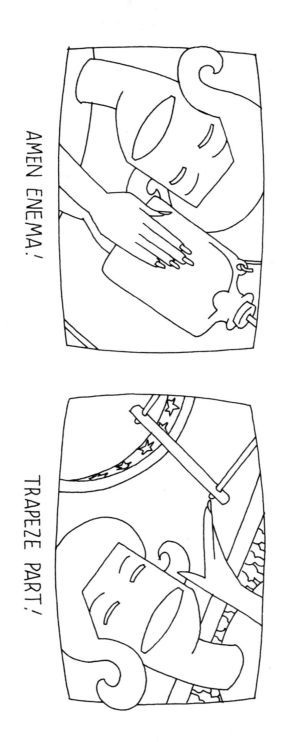

AMEN ENEMA!

TRAPEZE PART!

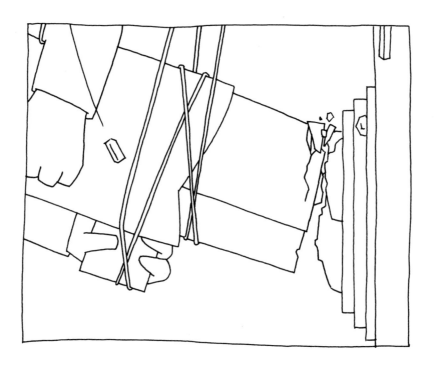

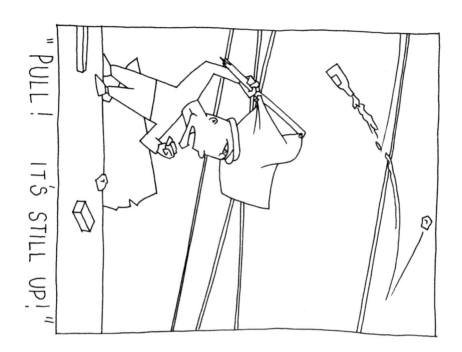

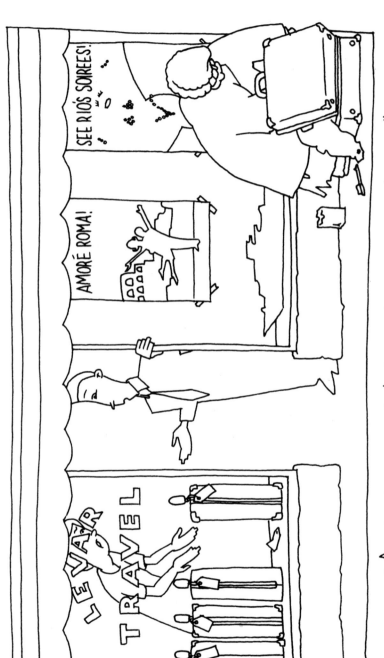

"A VAGABOND — A HOBO — HAD NO BAG, AVA."

LIVES DROWN IN WORDS EVIL.

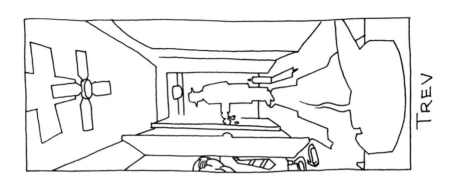

CIGAR

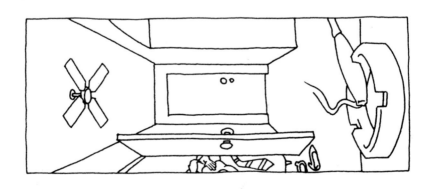

TREV

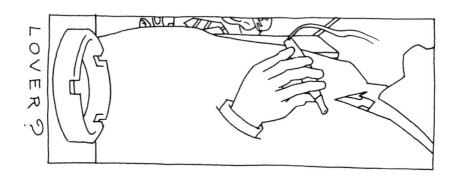

LOVER?

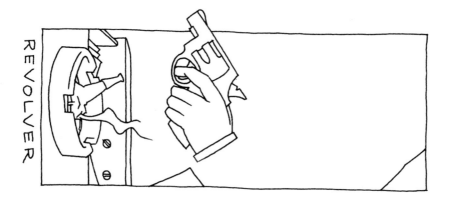

REVOLVER

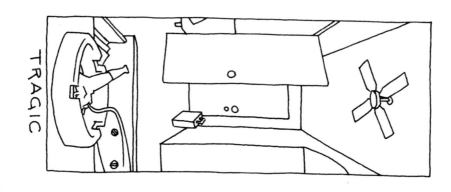

TRAGIC

PET SOW TWO-STEP

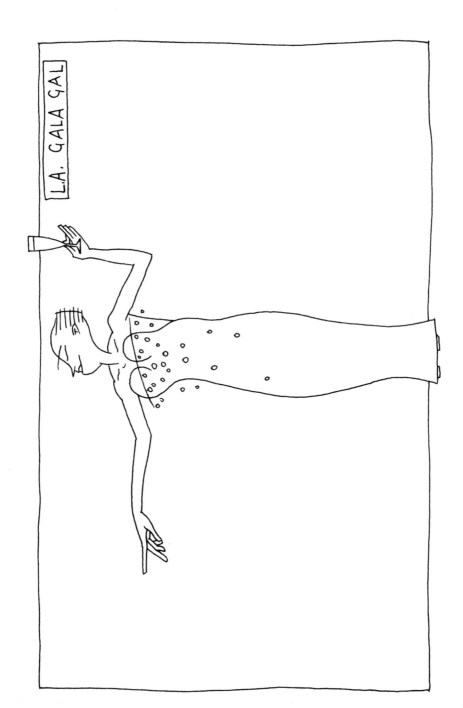

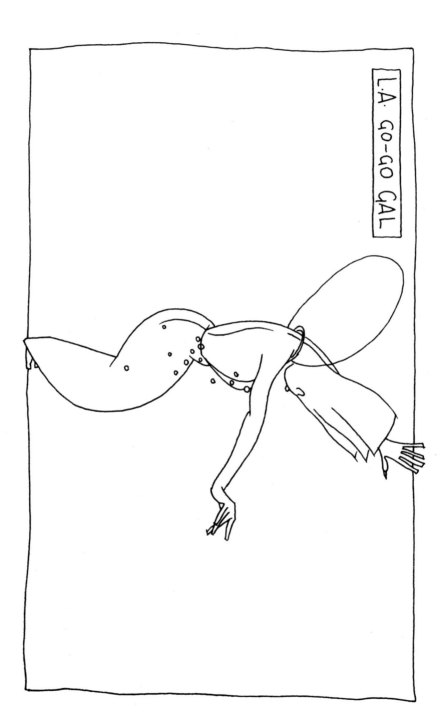

"DELIA, HER ASTRAL ARTS ARE HAILED!"

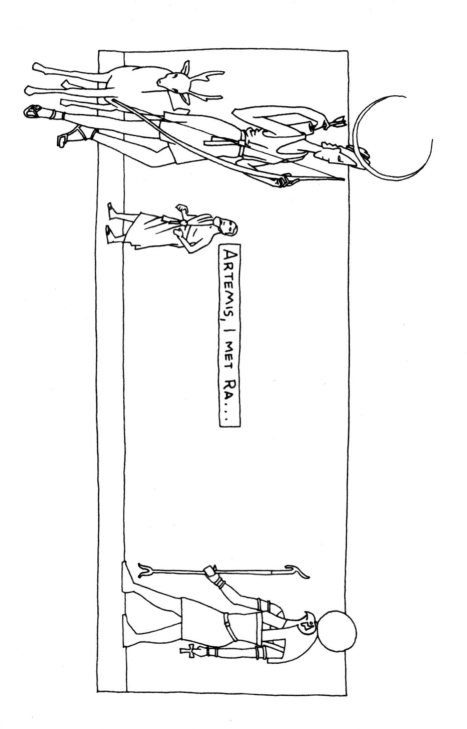

ARTEMIS, I MET RA...

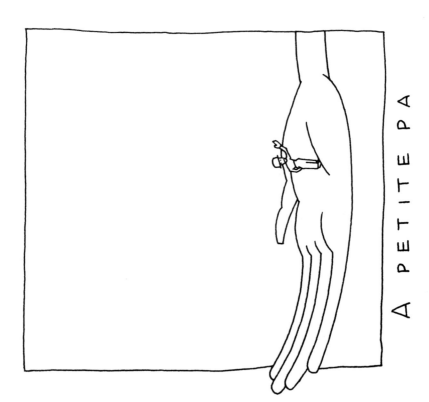

À PETITE PA

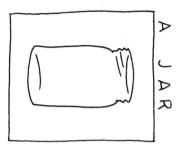

A JAR

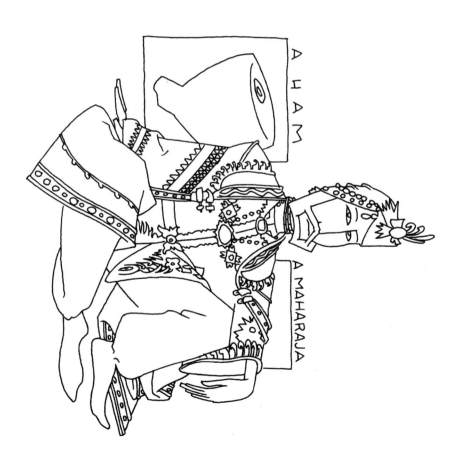

A HAM

A MAHARAJA

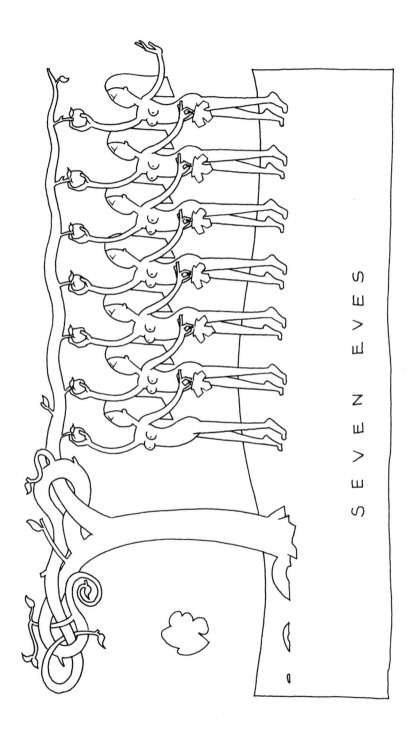

SEVEN EVES

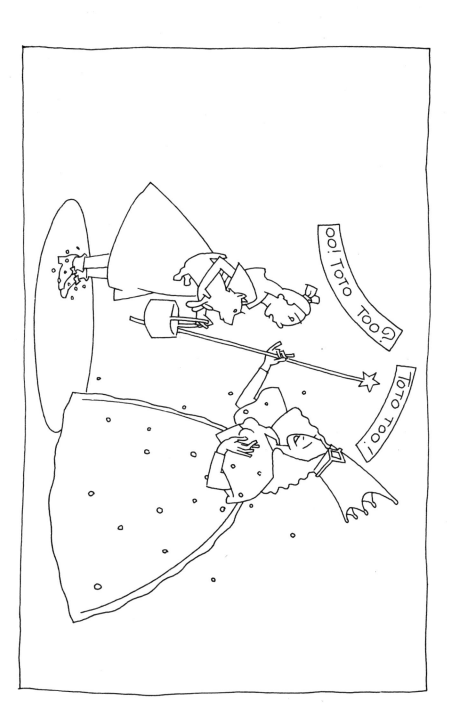

" NELL, EDNA, ARA, SAM — MEET NADENE, RAY, NAT, ANN, AHAB, ERIC, ART, ANA, TIM, MAT, LEON, BOB, MIKE, KIM, BOB, NOEL, TAMM', TANA, TRACI, REBA, HANNA, TANYA, RENE, DANTE, EMMA, SARA, AND ELLEN."

film *Road to Life*, directed by Nikolai Ekk. The phrase "the pineapple of politeness" in footnote 73 is drawn from a line by the character Mrs. Malaprop in Richard Brinsley Sheridan's 1775 play *The Rivals*. Footnote 85 is a quote from Richard Bruce Nugent's "Smoke, Lilies and Jade," which was first published in the 1926 issue of *Fire!!*. Footnote 100 is a compressed quote from W. E. B. Du Bois's *The Souls of Black Folk*; the reference to the "dark and pierced Jew" in footnote 49 is drawn from the same book. I learned the parable of Moses and the lost sheep from my dear friend Josh Weiner. Angela Brentlinger and David Shneer both helped out with the fragments of Russian interspersed throughout the novel. Some of the weirder 1930s slang ("rhino suds," e.g.) came from the "Slang of the 30s" page on a site called Paper Dragon. The detail about boiled puffins in Iceland was drawn from Leni Zumas's marvelous novel *Red Clocks*. The scene in which the women of Zatelsk "let dance in the pan just a few pinches of sorrel and a snippet of thyme or two" is a tribute to a detail in a short story in which the contemporary protagonist does something similar with onions, but—Marx in himl forgive me—I cannot remember which story it is, or by whom, or when I read it, even; I am indebted to that author and text. Part of the Phonye's monologue in the early parts of the "philadelphiye" section is one of a few instances of deliberate anachronism, and is based on the transcript of an interview Claude Lanzmann did with the former first lieutenant of Einsatzgruppe C, Karl Kretschmer, for the film *Shoah*. Parts of this section (and others) reference the story of Sholem Schwartzbard's 1926 assassination of Simon Petlura. The phrase "o wa" was drawn from I. L. Peretz's *Stories and Pictures*, and from David Pinski's *Yiddish Tales*, also translated by Helena Frank. Comrade Bear-Meerkat's recitation at the CP meeting is a partial amalgamation of the poem "Lynching," by Barysh Vaynshteyn, and the poem "Strange Fruit," by Abel Meeropol. Charles's poem, "america," contains references to Osip Mandelstam's poem "The Stalin Epigram," also known as "The Kremlin Highlander," and to Anna Margolin's poem "langzam un likhtik," or "Unhurried and Radiant" in Ruth Whitman's translation, which is referenced a few other times throughout this novel. The character of Anna Trunksboym is a tribute to three Annas: the poet Anna Margolin (Clara Lebensboym), the writer and political activist Anna Strunsky, and my great-great-grandmother Anna Land. The phrase "Here goes, then" is a tribute to Etty Hillesum and her collected writings, published as *An Interrupted Life* and translated by Arnold J. Pomerans, which begins with the same phrase.

Zatelsk is a fictional village, but it is firmly located in the Volhynia region of northeastern Ukraine, somewhere near the center of a triangle formed by Lutsk, a midpoint between Rivne and Zhytomyr, and Pinsk, Belarus. Its location is significant in terms of both its geopolitical history and its dialectal nuances, and was determined in consultation with Rob Adler Peckerar, who also helped me come up with its name, which is an amalgam of Slavic and Yiddish, and which means something along the lines of beyond (Ukrainian/Slavic preface "za") catastrophe (Hebrew/Yiddish "tel"). Other physical and spiritual features of Zatelsk are based on the shtetl of Uzlyany, in central Belarus, where my great-great-grandparents were born, and where I was lucky to spend a time-bending, heart-changing morning, alongside folks from the Helix Fellowship in the summer of 2019. The trees on the cover of this book are based on a stand of trees in Uzlyany.

Printed in the USA
CPSIA information can be obtained
at www.ICGtesting.com
LVHW092327250224
772790LV00006B/353

9 781250 872166